Commodities Trading For Beginners

Commodity Trading Tips To Earn High Profits.

By: Priyank Gala

Published By:

Priyank Gala

©Copyright 2015 – : Priyank Gala

ISBN-13: 978-1517599102
ISBN-10: 1517599105

Table of Contents

Chapter 1: Defining Commodities

Any item which can be sold or purchased and has some value or assessment to it defines a commodity. Commodities cater to universal market by getting goods and services satisfied, in terms of a substance or any other thing, which can be purchased or sold in economic terms. Existence on this planet is not easy, and to improve this existence and living life, commodities play a vital role in helping people as being raw materials for sustaining in this world.

Two categories of Commodities have been created in order to understand and differentiate between different commodities, i.e. Soft Commodities (commodities which are cultivated/ agriculture) and hard commodities (mined commodities).

Commodity is used as an instrument for investment if investment landscape is taken as the context, but it has to be categorized into three different dimensions, which are:

1. **Tradable:** This means, under the supervision of a marketplace where goods are exchanged and is specific to its criteria's or for exchange, commodities as instruments for investments can be bought or sold. Exchange Traded Funds (ETFs) are used to track the fund price movements in some cases, whereas future transactions need to be covered by specially designed underlying future contracts for commodities, in consideration with the practices of investments in today's league.

2. **Physically Deliverable:** Commodities, which can be processed and delivered in the physical state rather than using, cash for transactions are under these commodities.

3. **With High Liquidity Levels:** These commodities are tradable and the volume of sales for these are exceptionally high with a huge market where the potential of getting buyers for every seller and vice-versa is easy, thus making it easier for the investors to enter or leave the market according to their wish.

It is important to note that it is not a single country, which is catered to; rather these commodities, which act as the building blocks of the nation, serve the entire world. Energy (oil, coal or natural gas help in deriving energy for better living), Metals (gold, uranium, silver & steel are precious metals used for making various products like weapons, tools, jewelry or even act as solid substance for liquid money) and Agricultural products (food) are the three categories these commodities are diversified into.

Commodity exchanges started establishing all around the world, which were very similar to CBOT, because global economies were being derived majorly with the role commodities played for this role. Every individual exchange has a single or a few selected commodities with a specialization in them. There are more than 50 commodity exchanges around the world in today's date, with the famous ones as:

- **Commodity Exchange Inc./ COMEX** (merger in 1994 led to this getting under the division of New York Mercantile Exchange now) deals with precious metals like gold and silver as their primary market.

- **New York Mercantile Exchange/ NYMEX** (part of Intercontinental Exchange/ICE), which ensures itself as the primary market for Crude Oil & Natural Gas, i.e., WTI *West Texas Light Sweet) but in partnership with ICE.

- **Intercontinental Exchange/ ICE**, plays a vital role for being the primary market for Sugar No. 11 & 14, also for WTI Crude and Brent Crude, rather in other words, a network which is globally connected for commodity exchanges and has the rights of ownership for around the world clearing houses and different commodity exchanges.

- **Chicago Board of Trade/ CBOT**(Chicago Mercantile Exchange Group Member) acts as the concerned and main market of coffee and corn as the agricultural products.

- **London Metal Exchange** acts as the industrial metals primary market.

- **Multi Commodity Exchange** (India based), amongst the highest rates 10 exchange commodities around the globe for products like silver, natural gas, and gold.

- **Tokyo Commodity Exchange**, products like rubber, crude oil and precious metals are the products for which futures trading is regulated in Japan.

The commodity prices are not determined or set by the commodity exchanges. The only function of commodity exchanges are to give the facilities of communication systems in order to facilitate information dissemination and price reporting, and also acts as a platform for selling and buying by traders. Abiding by the rules of exchange and regulations of commodity trading, set by the federal government is necessary, and thus employees are assigned to oversee the operations of this matter.

Fungibility

The process and ability to allow exchange or interchange between similar or identical assets is defined as Fungibility. Commodities first characteristic used for defining commodity is Fungibility.
Example: If we take Mixed fruit juices of A and B can be categorized under fungible products as in the end they are mixed juices and does not really matter where and how they were manufactured or cultivated. All that needs to be taken into consideration is that, they should be edible and ripe enough to consume and are set according to the standards of food and beverage division and is good to taste, they can be exchanged.

Another example of this is GOLD, irrespective of whether it is from London or Austria, as the purity levels are same and can be used under Fungibility. Does not make a difference as to who's gold is it, in the end it would be sold at the gold rate f the market.

Due to the characteristic of Fungibility, it is easier for trading of commodities like gold, natural gas, oil or mixed juice in high volume at the same price.

External Factors with Commodities

As we know now that one of the main essences of defining a commodity is Fungibility. External factors like weather also play as high commodity investments. As an example, if crops like tea are destroyed due to a hurricane over a place, then the person who is a commodity investor has the rights to purchase crops as much as they want. Therefore, with the correct judgment of the fact that finally the prices of these crops would take a hike and benefits would be seen.

Liquidity

Commodities' trading has liquidity as a very critical aspect. Exchange of each commodity is made in the markets where buyers and sellers are present for trading regularly. The need of having a buyer or seller is not necessary for a commodity investor when they have liquidity with them, thus can enter or leave at their own will.

Speculators present under commodities adding more value to the market by providing liquidities, thus earning some profits, can assume the risk of price fluctuation. Years of existence of this trading method have been seen. Now, let's see what the history is for this market, as now the basic concept of commodities is known.

Chapter 2: Commodities as an Investment Vehicle

Methods of investment like bonds, savings account, stock trading and option lack at advantages as and when compared to the advantages of Commodities when used as an investment vehicle. Gaining huge profits within small time frames are the best and the main component of commodity trading. Understanding the part of leverage in foreign traded currencies and the feasibility of this type of feat is easier when trading of foreign exchange currencies has been made.

Having the expectation of earning high-profit amounts by using the borrowed capital is called leverage in the financial market. In simple words, commodities futures contract which might turn up to be profitable up to 10x of the initial amount can be bought with a small capital investment. Even the slightest price change in the futures market can lead to high losses or high profits. Thus, the leverage can have both good and bad impact on a person, just like a sharp double-sided knife.

Due to the established initial margins by the exchanges, highest leverage is seen with trading in commodities futures market when compared to the other investment options. The contracts are pretty high as compared to the investment margins. Thus, proving that futures market is high at risk and are also very useful. The leverage would be greater when the margin level is small in relativeness to the each commodities futures contract cash value.

Example: If an amount of $15,000 is present in a trading account of a commodities futures investor, and an investment in a contract, which has an index value of 1300 at present for a long term position, and the value of contract is $350 times the index specified ($350 * 1300 = $455,000), thus a profit of loss of $250 will be seen over every point lost or gained in the index.

Now, within a time frame of 6 months, if an index gain of total 6.5% is seen, it would mean that an increase of 84.5 points of the index in order to equal 1385 (round figured). Now, when looking at the monetary side, a gain of $21,125 (84.5 points * $250) will be seen as an investor of commodity futures. Thus, a return of 141% is seen as compared to the investment.

From a different perspective, a loss of $21,125 will be seen if the index shows a decrease of 6.5%, which is pretty high as compared to the initial investment. Now, as an assumption, we are sure that you can see that even after the depletion of the account, some amount of $6,125 is left, which has to be paid by the investor. The risk factor of large profits or losses with even a small percentage of fluctuation is an add-on element that is seen with leverage.

The potential probability of gaining huge profits within a small time frame is what drives investors into this field of commodities futures market, thus this being the initial advantage that can be seen on financial investment vehicles when compared to the commodities futures.

Low commissions are another advantage of commodities futures when used as an investment vehicle. A commission of $40- $60 would have to be paid for a profit of $21, 125. Commission close to 1% has to be paid for both sales and purchases for individual stocks, whereas an expenditure of thousands and thousands of dollars would have been made for the purpose of selling or purchase of a stock batch.

It is important to understand that every decision made in commodity trading is not always correct and is an evident factor; rather making the right decision as to what should be bought or sold is very difficult.

A significant advantage can be seen while commodities speculation as compared to the various other investment vehicles, which are non-liquid, i.e. real estate. The trading account balance is readily available and handy whenever it is needed. Spending profits earned on an open trade is available when a particular margin is maintained without any change to the position, whereas withdrawing assets is not acceptable or possible without selling them off in other investment vehicles like bonds and the stocks.

Let's continue to learn commodity trading while learning the complete commodities futures trading background and understand that the complexity of the trading process is not as high as it is said to be. There are only 40 futures market in the commodities market which can be used for trading, whereas more than 1000 potential aspects are available for trade in other markets like stock exchange, which respectively span the various world economy sectors and areas.

Irrespective of the increase or decrease in value, the ability to make profits is seen in commodities trading when used as an investment vehicle. Taking advantage of any evident scenario of the economy is possible with a diversified portfolio of the futures markets. Irrespective of depression in the economy or its boom, or even any other reasons like famines, war, winters or various natural calamities, the opportunity is always present with commodity trading.

As a commodities trader, some tax advantages are offered with futures trading. Automatic taxation of 60% and 40% is made for long term and short tern gains respectively, regardless of the holding period. The rate of 33% at the highest is made on the profits, which when compared to average individual income's highest rate, comes out to be really low. Commodity trading definitely benefits incase reestablishment is seen for the long-term profit rates to be lower than the short-term profit rates.

As an investment vehicle, commodities futures market trading is an excellent option. Even though there are risks involved, earning profits of approximately thousands of dollars for the investors due to the advantages it has to offer. Before heading further with the advantages of commodities futures trading, it is important to understand the risks involved in-depth.

Chapter 3: Gold & Silver

Gold and Silver Trading

The most popular investment vehicles in precious metals are Gold and Silver. These precious metals are considered to be a safe option of investment and prove to be an excellent support during various situations of crisis whether social, economical or political due to the intrinsic value present with them.

Facts about Gold

A total world production estimation of approximately 2,520 tons is seen with Gold, and the primary source of its production is through mining. In 1970, South Africa proved to be the leader in Gold production with the ratio of 80% accountability in the world production for Gold, which makes it almost half of the world's total gold reserve. But by the year 2007, with 276 metric tons of gold production, China overtook South Africa leading produce, which is after the time period when the decline to just 10% of the usual production output (or 272 metric tons) was seen by South Africa.

There are more than 40 gold markets all over the world located at different international financial centers where trading of Gold is done, where the most influential is the London Gold Market amongst them. The trading of gold around the world depends on the London Gold Fixing, which is done at 10:30 a.m. and 3:00 p.m. every day, thus being the benchmark in this case. The Global Gold Market framework is formed by more than 40 gold markets.

Following factors are the reasons for fluctuation on gold prices:

- *The inflationary pressures presence* – the moment acceleration is seen in the price, gold attracts the capital flight.

- *Dwindling production*– it has become difficult to dig for gold and the digging has to be done deeper to acquire gold, thus giving a rise to the mining costs, thus reducing the supply. A gold consumption estimate of 3,500 is seen whereas the gold production on an average is at 2,500; thus it is still a big question as to how and where the production of the remaining 1,000 metric tons of Gold can be achieved.

- **Demands for Gold Reserves** –the highest gold buyers are the central banks of various countries. An impact will be seen on the various gold markets due to any activity of gold buying by these banks.
- **Demand of Investors**–Gold prices at nay given time can be impacted with speculative interest or dis-interest in gold.

Investing in Gold

Gold investment can be made in various ways, be it buying gold coins, any physical form of gold, jewelry or even physical gold or buying gold mining companies stock shares. Spot Gold Prices (Gold ETFs) can be tracked by Exchange Traded Funds present, which can easily be included in the portfolio of investment.

Through commodity exchanges like COMEX or New York Mercantile Exchange, purchase and selling of gold futures is the most popular as well as the convenient way of investment. Trading can be done directly with the exchange or online via regular brokers and virtual trading platforms respectively.

Online trading is advisable rather than opening a direct trading account with the exchange, for the retail investors due to less capital requirement, along with the benefit of longer hours for trading.

Opening an online account with a member of broker change is all that is needed to start gold futures trading. Any online broker that is accredited by the Globex, CME, DGCX of Dubai, NCDEX of India, Tokyo Commodity Exchange or Multi Commodity Exchange can be used as options in case of Gold. A virtual trading platform linked with the real-time global gold market is provided once an account holder, thus giving the benefit of purchasing gold futures or spot prices trading of gold in real time which have the requirements of minimal margin can be achieved.

Metatrader 4 is used as the virtual platform by most of the online brokers due to its popularity and user-friendliness, which allows trading of either of the serviced securities by just a single account with the broker-provider. A powerful array of real-time financial news feed and technical arrays is seen by this trading platform, in order to make trading decisions less difficult.

Trading in lots, which are equivalent to 100 ounces of gold is done for Gold Futures (including spot gold or current month). Micro or e-mini accounts are also offered by some brokers which are relatively smaller in size with 10 ounces and 1 ounces per lot is seen compared to the regular accounts of 100ounces per lot.

A ticker symbol of GC is seen with Nymex Gold while ECG is the electronic trading counterpart under CME, which has a ticker symbol of MGC.

The notional value of contracts with the low margins as 1% makes trading as highly leveraged, although the highest maximum leverage of 1:1000 is for gold micro account. The leverage margin trading of 1:50 has been limited to by the current regulation in the U.S. A minimum $0.10 per ounce price increments and 10ounces of micro accounts in the contract size is noticed, with 40% of the notional value has been set as the margin call with 10% NV (Notional Value – No. Of ounces x current price/106) is the automatic cut point. For every position, which is taken, $2000 is needed as the initial margin requirement for regular accounts.

Gold Outlook Currently

Since the last 2.5 years, the prices of gold have been plummeting, with a loss of 27% of the value, and further drop from the high of $1,923.70 per ounce at September 2011.This extreme price drop is due to the improvement in the U.S. and global economies as the main contributing factors, which changed the way of investments into meaningful options and outlook instead of staying in the safe haven. However, a question that arises here is that after reaching the bottom with 2.5 years of stormy down trend, is another rally ready to be mounted?
Due to the demand-supply equation of gold, its luster and trust has been lost amongst the investors and they would take time to invest much into gold easily again. The short gold supply, would definitely grab the market again soon, due to the constant demand for it.

The gold supply crunch due to a supply dropping by 3% is expected to stay till 2014, thus which might increase and trigger the gold trend upwards.

Although, exhaustive analysis of the price movements currently should be done before the bottom picking, which is tricky.

Facts about Silver

As an investment specifically and also otherwise, in many aspects, silver is just like gold. The market liquidity is 18times lower than gold, thus making the silver price movement volatile. Thus, the profound impact can be seen on prices of silver with even the slightest single volume transactions. An even worse scenario is that movement of silver prices can be influenced by large traders or investors. A ratio of 1:50 gold/silver is seen under normal market conditions of silver tracking gold prices.

A mere $15.2 billion per year is estimated for physical silver demand, whereas, the uses of silver in industries is on a high with almost all industrial, consumer and commercial products with the silver-based biocides, which use the particles of Nano-silver with various applications including the dressing of wounds, masks for surgeries, bone cement, and also home appliances silver particles.

A ticker symbol of SI of regular silver futures is seen with 5,000 ounces per lot contract size, requiring $11,000 as an initial margin deposit and $10,000 as the maintenance margin requirements.
A ticker symbol of SIL has been given to micro silver future with just 1,000 ounces per lot as the contract size and $2,200 per lot as the initial margin requirement with $2,000 as the maintenance margin requirement.

Outlook of Silver

It is believed by the analysts that due to shedding of 35% of its value since 2013 mid-December, silver will have just a little appetite, even though the industrial sector has high demand for it. Even though gold prices are also in the doldrums, silver would keep tracking its prices.

Chapter 4: Oil

Crude oil is extracted from deep inside the ground by drilling oil wells underneath the individual natural rock formations, which are needed as the source for Crude Oil. Refinement into petroleum products like petrol, gasoline, kerosene, liquefied petroleum gas, etc. needs to be done once the crude oil extraction is done in order to get the maximum benefit of crude oil, which can be achieved only by this method.

Due to the fact that majority of investors in crude oil futures are either direct buyers, sellers or producers, aiming and hoping for purchase and sale at price which is advantageous in order to not let volatile price movements affect them, crude oil futures prove themselves to be just the perfect contracts amongst the sellers and buyers. Speculators wishing to get advantages with prices going up are also present with crude oil futures.

On looking at the investment landscape, one of the most transparent and liquid markets is the crude oil market, and amongst the trading done around the entire world for all the physical commodities, the largest futures contract lies with crude oil. Also, the maximum derivative products available are with crude oil futures.

Trading of Crude Oil futures at NYMEX are:

- **Brent Crude Oil Futures**(ticker symbol BB) has 1,000 barrels per lot as the contract size (1 barrel- 42 gallons). A minimum price fluctuation of $0.01 per barrel is the quoted price in USD, with $10 plus or minus the closing of the day before daily price movement limit. Per lot maintenance margin of $3,700 and $4,070 as the initial margin requirement is seen.

- **Light Sweet Crude Oil Futures** (ticker symbol CL), with the specifications which are the same as seen and noticed with Brent Crude, although the difference lies with $3,400 per lot as the maintenance margin requirement and $3,740 as the initial margin requirement.

Following Micro contracts are seen with the above mentioned crude oil futures:

Micro Brent Crude Oil Futures (ticker symbol MBZ), 1Barrel per lot (42 Gallons) as the contract size. It has per lot requirements of $3 as maintenance margin, $4 as initial margin and $0.01 as the minimum price fluctuations.

Micro Crude Oil Futures (ticker symbol MCL) has the same requirements for the initial and maintenance margins and also has contract specifications, which are similar to that of Micro Brent Crude Oil.

Supply side factors determine and dictate the crude oil prices. The oil deposits of the top 5 Middle Eastern countries, i.e. Saudi Arabia, Qatar, Kuwait, Iraq, and UAE have 62% of the oil supply around the world. Amongst these five countries, two countries are not full-fledged into the production of crude oil as due to protracted wars in Iraq and the same natural gas fields are seen with the Qatar oil-wells.

Secondly, depletion of earth's natural oil deposits has also been theorized. As early as 1956, M. King Hubbert, a geophysicist predicted the depletion of oil production by reaching its peak and flattening thereafter and then go on the level of decline, and as early as 1970, this peak has been reached according to the prediction made by him.

An upward direction or path will be seen in the prices of crude oil until new resources, alternative energy sources or oil fields are discovered for tapping crude oil.

Chapter 5: Corn, Coffee, Sugar

Commodities grown in contrast to the mined hard commodities are called the 'Soft commodities', and Corn, Sugar and Coffee under these 'Soft Commodities.' The godfather of the investment markets is the agricultural commodities market, due to its long present history.

The challenges of vulnerability to diseases, insects, weather pattern changes, etc. to the agriculture and cultivation done by the farmers, have been around ever since the start and prevailed even today. The producers' and buyers' face havoc due to the price volatility due to these factors seen in the supply and demand plus the weather changes, which are unforeseen.

The farmer's through commodity futures can lock in the selling price of crops while the same opportunity of profitable prices to get in are present with the buyers. A massive level of opportunities is given to the speculators to get profits with volatility of the market.

Commodity trading obviously has two sides to a coin, where someone's gain would result in someone else's loss, thus, gaining and losing fortunes is a part of trading in commodities. If the basic knowledge of every agricultural commodity future, which a person trades in, the risks involved in it can be mitigated with commodity trading even if the investor is not on the winning side.

Coffee-Contract Specification:

Coffee is traded with prices quoted in US cents per pound and the trading is done in lots, with 37,500 Pounds of coffee in each lot, plus $0.0005 per pound minimum fluctuations and the ticker symbol TK. March, May, July, September and December are the months to which the contract months are limited and 83,850 per lot is the initial margin requirement with $3,500 per lot as the requirement for minimum maintenance margin.

Coffee Outlook:

Due to the low supply and increase in global demand, the coffee prices are expected by traders to raise by 2014. The Arabica coffee prices have lowered down with around 52% as compared to the raise it saw in 2011.Although, further downside momentum will be stalled as the speculative short positions load the coffee market for the 2013-14 planting season with the deficit of the potential production.

Sugar:

Sugar is traded with prices quoted in US cents per pound and the trading is done in lots, with 112.000 Pounds in each lot, plus $0.0001 per pound minimum fluctuations, per contract equivalent to $11.20. Sugar #11 is traded by NYMEX, with YO as its ticker symbol, having $3,500 per lot as the margin requirement for minimum maintenance and $3,850 per lot as the initial margin requirement. March, May, July, and October are the months limited as contract months.

Sugar Outlook:

Although no change is seen in the consumption estimate, the sugar supply was cut down by 94,000 tons short because of the Louisiana's production falling short in the fiscal year 2013/14 as the U.S. supply of sugar projected. However, with the bumper crops in India and Brazil, an increase by 2% is slated with sugar production. Along with this, it is predicted by the experts that the developing countries particularly will also show high rise in consumption of sugar.

Corn:

Trading of corn is done in lots, with 5,000 bushels in each lot, which is 127 metric tons of a rough estimate. ¼ of 1 cent per bushel, equivalent to $12.50 per contract is the minimum price fluctuation seen with the quoted prices in U.S. cents per bushel, $2,363 per lot as the initial margin, $1,750 per lot as the minimum margin of maintenance and ticker symbol as C for corn futures. March, May, July, September and December as the contract months for corn.

Corn Outlook:

Due to the increase in feed and ethanol production, corn consumption for the fiscal year 2013/14 is estimated to rise. A short and tight corn supply for the present year is possible with the estimation of ending stocks of corn to be as low as 161 million bushels.

The Bottom Line:

A prudent and a wise move to diversify are adding the agricultural commodities to the portfolio, which offers the potential of an upward trend and downside protection if done properly. Let's learn the meaning of binary options and the way online trading is done through them, before further details on using binary options for commodity trading are discussed.

Chapter 6: Commodity Trading with Binary Options

Knowing about binary options is a rare thing, and maybe one must not have known about it before going through this book. The perfect commodity-trading tool is binary options due to the high volatility of the commodity markets.

Binary options are pretty simple in terms of use, and it is easy to understand them, thus make a place amongst one of the simplest financial instruments for trading. Foreign exchange markets, indices, commodities, and stocks hold the base for trading of binary options. Due to the option of fixed expiry date/time and strike price, binary options also hold the name as a fixed-return option. The purchase of binary options as a "call" or a "put" option can be bought.

A "Call" option:

The "Call" option can be defined in terms of winning and losing depending on the strike price at the moment when the binary option is supposed to expire. Thus the trader loses if the strike price is lower during the expiry moment, whereas if the strike price is higher at the expiry moment, the trader wins.

A "Put" option:

On purchase of the "put" option, the investor wins if the price is lower than the strike price during the expiry moment. The investor loses if the strike price at the moment is higher than the price.

Winning and Losing a Trade:

There are two terms used under this category called the "being in the money" and "being out of the money", which respectively mean being wrong side of the strike price and being on the right side of the strike price. In consideration to the price movements, being in the money and out of the money is possible in trade. Winning and losing a trade is defined by the final price during the expiry time.

Irrespective of the amount won with binary option trade, a fixed amount is returned back, whereas the invested amount is the loss seen when losing a binary option trade, or it might be a percentage of it that is faced as a loss, which is completely in the hands of the broker.

Example:

Lets assume, the binary options is not bothered whether the investor can figure out the price of the gold stock which might go up, when the analysts say that according to the gold market charts, the gold prices would increase. Thus, the investor decides on purchase of a call binary option for gold with the broker, which is present at $1235,355 market price at present, plus the investor wishes to invest $50, a payout of 80% is offered by the broker on winning the trade, also losing this amount is also there on losing the trade.

Now, investment of $50 in call option is decided as per the market analysis, which shows that the gold prices will show a small upward movement of price. Thus, further ahead if the expiry of binary trade option expired when it is higher than $1235,355 as the strike price, the investment and the winning, i.e. $50 + $40(winning) = $90 will be paid back by the broker.

Now, let's say that the price is lower than the strike price at the moment of expiry; the investment of $50 is lost. Moreover, if the price is same as the strike price of the expiry moment, this makes the investor get a return of the investment made without any further amendments, i.e. $50.

Now binary options are clear and further discussions can be made on using the commodities markets for trade, along with getting profits with the binary and commodities markets together. As discussed before, high volatility is seen in the commodities markets, i.e. short period of time sees a large number of price movements. Due to these short expiry times, advantages of this can be taken with binary options. Adding to this, the right direction of the trade matters, with which the up and down movement of the price does not really make a difference or matter.

A demo or an original account would be needed with the Forex broker in order to get started, thus to handle the MT4 program charts and quotes which will be needed for analyzing the commodities of choice. The MT4 software can be downloaded from http:/www.alpri.co.uk/demo for free. A free demo account would have to be created once the MT4 software is downloaded, also within a timeframe of 5 minutes, appropriate charts would also have be opened. It is important to know how setting up charts and finishing them is done. Thus it can be learned from http://www.binarvoptionsuniversitv.net/get- charts / if a person is new to this.

Now, the chart software needed for an account with the broker of binary options is ready, and Stock pair would be the best broker for this strategy. The account with Stock pair can be created at http://tinyurl.com/karevvt. CiTrades can be used as an alternate for trading, and the sign-up can be done at http://tinyurl.com/kmrsz6ior Trader XP, which can be downloaded at http://tinyurl.com/mnvr68z. Both of these are equivalently good with withdrawal's, which are fast and have nice payouts.

Now, since the requirements are ready, i.e. chart software and binary options broker, the setting up of the charts is required with the indicators, which are correct for the trading to initiate. The indicators which are necessary have been collected and put on http://www.binaryoptionsuniversity.net/downloads/commodities-binary.rar for further use, thus to save some time on it.

Once the file is downloaded, the .rar file can be extracted into the installed MT4 software's directory.
Opening the chart for commodity trading after restarting the MT4 software is the next step. Although, gold is the recommended commodity for trading, any other commodity is also fine for this strategy. Now, lets learn the strategy with keeping gold as the preferred choice of commodity. Through the MT$ software, click on the XAU/USD pair through the symbols screen located at the top left side of the software, now right click on the pair, then choose the chart window through it, to open a gold chart. Thus, a new window with the gold chart will be opened. Now, the whole thing is set, once the timeframe is set to around 5 minutes. Next step is to select a template by right clicking on the chart, but it should be remembered that a template with the name "trx-improved' would be present and should be selected, which would automatically change the screen into a picture which somewhat resembles the below picture:

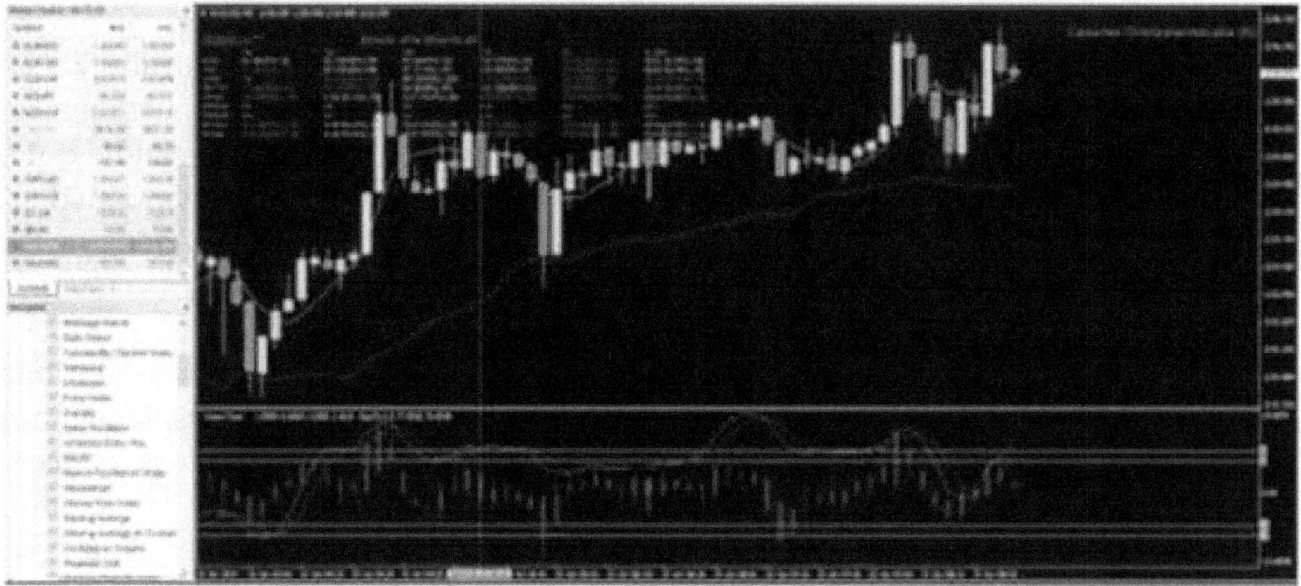

This chart might look complex, whereas it is quite simple to understand the strategy here. Now, lets discuss the step-by-step process in the chart, before learning to take the right trade decision with combining the indicators needed for the first trade.

The Neuron BO TRX Indicator

The first indicator to be seen on the screen is this. The lines around the prices, which are in blue and red, are what show the Neuron BO TRX indicator, also price movement outside this line is seen at times, thus the wait for this will be needed for making the strategy work. Thus, one of the three primary and most important indicators for a trade to be possible is to wait for the prices to move under the red line or over the blue line.

The Value Chart 2 Indicator

The second basic and important indicator is this amongst the three. The values of the value charts have to be more than +8 or less than -8 for the valid trade signals. Although +6 r -6 also allows the signal to be valid, but with higher risks. Thus, the wait and patience is needed unless either of these levels is achieved, and the yellow lines in the below image indicate the levels.

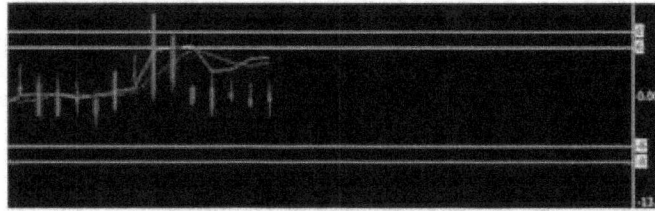

The value chart levels are indicated by the yellow lines

The Stochastic Indicator

The third of the main indicators is this, i.e. the Stochastic Indicator. The light blue and red lines seen at the screen bottom, at the Value chart2 window, which follow the prices are these indicators. The red line has to be crossed by the blue line in either direction, whether upwards or downwards, only then a valid signal is achieved. The other two indicators should be taken into consideration, and all three factors should be in the same direction for the trade to be successful.

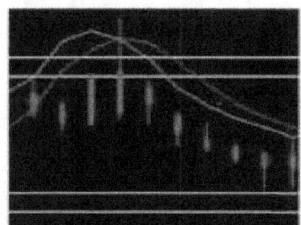

The blue line crosses the red line indicating a potential trade

FXTrend indicator is the last and final indicator, and the function of this si to validate the market trends and holds no importance in checking the validity of trade. This indicator ensures the correct view of the upward and downward trend of the market.

Time to Place a Trade

Now, we know that the money making a part is being awaited to be learned about, now is the time we would learn about it. As mentioned before, before placing a trade, all the three indicators should be taken into consideration, as the perfect trade situation can be seen through the image below, with the correct markings of all the three indicators needed.

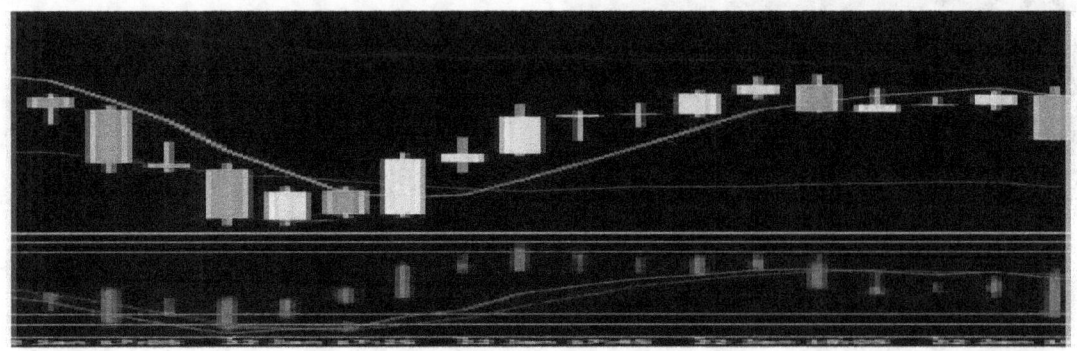

The blue stochastic line crosses the red line, the indicator level +8 is being crossed through the value chart 2 and the upward trend is seen with the prices outside the Neuron Lines. An easy winning trade would have been achieved if the investment were made in a put trade with 5-10minutes from the entry time as the expiry, although there would have been no problem with a longer time even.

But short expiries, with commodities specially is suggested with this strategy because huge price movements with short time durations would be seen to the maximum extent.

Trade Example 2: Good Trade

The time to give the right signals by all the indicators is just a few minutes, in the second example above. But, it is seen easily that on placing a call trade, winning some money easily was possible.

It is important to remember that the rules of this strategy need to be followed for gaining profits. The trade should be skipped if all the three indicators together re not giving the green signal.

Trade Example 3: Bad Trade

Look at the above image to understand things. The price was outside the Neuron BO TRX red line and the indicator was below -8 for the value chart 2, but the crossing of the stochastic lines was not yet seen. Thus, if the trade were placed in this strategy, losses would have been faced at nearly every moment of expiry.

Trading in this strategy can be summarized now, with remembering that the green signal should be seen from all the three indicators, and not even a single of them should miss it. It is always better to trade within 5-20minutes from the entry time. The trade is better skipped, and the wait for a new setup is better if the broker does not have the right expiry time. Stock pair helps avoid this problem as with this, setting up of own expiry times is possible.

Remember, http://tinyurl.com/karg5vt helps with opening an account with Stock pair.

Chapter 7: Path to proper Commodities Trading

The process of actually trading in the market can be discussed now since we have a complete understanding of the risks and benefits of commodity trading. Education is the initial step towards trading in commodities. The education here does not refer to the market history, but rather about education training; basically the knowledge needed for beginning the trade positions with the real money.

It is best to look for a trader who has established himself successfully in the market, and it is the most beneficial step for better trading. Due to the fact that the final goal is encompassed by them, a great deal of knowledge can be acquired by them due to the amount of wisdom they have in this field, along with being trained personally about how the trading takes place in the market and how they do it. The opportunity should never be wasted, if a trader who is ready to educate is available and give the patience and tie to teach. This will be the perfect way to learn things and get the required knowledge in the field of trading which can be achieved only by these professional traders, which would furthermore help in avoiding the common mistakes new traders make while trying to be successful in the market of commodities trading.

A combination of the acquired knowledge and gained experience in the market is what makes the perfect way for trading. It is not a sure shot thing that the same method of trading would work for both the mentor and the learner, as the capital and the experience of years into trading might be missing, which is necessary for professional trading. A progressive approach toward becoming a successful commodities trader can be achieved through developing a personal trading style and also implementing the knowledge characteristics gained from the mentors.

Demo Trading

The trial and error method is another way of developing the proper commodities trading way. Without investing in the real money, various strategies and styles of trading commodities can be practiced through a demo trading account, and is the most convenient way for beginners to learn without facing losses. Random reinforcement should also be taken into consideration despite of demo trading being one of the greatest methods for learning how to trade.

Thus, the trial and error in demo trading has downfalls, which mean that tons of profits and getting lucky is possible while trading like an idiot, or face loads of multiple losses through the use of some effective system while practicing trading on a demo account.

Now, this sounds like a contradicting statement, isn't it? Since, one side we say that a demo trading is an excellent option, and then we say that losses and idiotic investments can be made through it. Actually, this is the truth, it is not about contradicting here, rather the realistic approach is being shown here, to help the beginners fall prey to the trading pitfalls, which is a normal scenario with them.

Reading books is the best for countering the random reinforcements. Overcoming this trial and error methods downfall can be done through reading the tips, ideas or any books written by various authors who are well respected, going through online books and other written sources. Although, going through books and mugging them up also have downfalls of their own, just like the demo trading. The fact which holds that the things written in books, rarely make an impact while trading in commodities or generally do not work, although this is a very well kept secret from the readers.

Now, obviously reading this, it is a point to wonder what was just mentioned above.

It is pretty likely that while trading in the environment of live market, losses would be faced, despite of the trading strategies mentioned in the books by the authors who are well respected for their work despite of the fact that they look to be effective but fail eventually. The authors just talk about the trading strategies effectiveness being mentioned and not the side effects or downfalls it would have on the trader. The best way is to use some of the examples in various scenarios of the market and check what is effective and what incurs an accumulation of multiple losses.

So, how can trading be done in a proper way?

A lot of time and diligence is needed to learn the proper way of trading and not just learn in a week's time. An accumulation of the practical experiences gained through the live market tracking and the ideas and knowledge learned from it is what creates the perfect way of trading. A continuous approach should be made in learning the mistakes, which are seen in the live market by keeping a close watch of it, and they should be pondered upon every day at some decided time. No books or mentor can give the knowledge, which can be achieved through this gaining experience done.

Intelligence and practice are not the main qualities needed for proper trading, rather self-awareness of self-trading style, discipline, and emotional control hold the main grounds of proper trading. It is detrimental in providing a successful path in commodities trading when these paths are implicated and put into action. No scientific strategy, which a layman cannot understand and use, is not needed for learning to trade in the live markets.

The Occam's razor can be used for this purpose, which defines the fact that it is best to use the simplest way which can be effective in the market of trade is the right way rather than using a sophisticated strategy which might get more confusing later on and fails to deliver the results. Most of the effective trading strategies or plans have been the simplest of all. Trading is done in a simple yet a unique way by using and implementing all the necessary factors or proper trading, which is used through the Occam's razor's principle.

Chapter 8: Risk Trading Commodity Futures

Realistic approach as to what to trade with and which investment vehicle to use is needed when trading into commodities futures and not get too excited over it for the fact that we have learnt about the possible large profits in trading of commodities futures, since losses are also possible with commodity futures trading.

The surety of 100% winning every time trading is done, is something no strategy can give. A check on the reality is kept even by the professional traders in the market while making each and every trade, due to the fact that losses faced are pretty higher as compared to the winning streak of a trade, and this is something which every trader should understand.

We know by now the risk carried in trading of commodities futures due to the leverage, and also the fact that more money can be seen as a loss than the investment itself, thus making the investors shy away from such type of investments options. Rather, a pretty understandable fact here is that any naïve trader would refrain from the second attempt of investing with these risky trades.

What makes trading commodities future riskier than the other investments?

Based on the investment, an exposure to nearly unlimited liabilities is given by trading of commodities futures, which is a contrast to the limited amount of losses seen in the stock market or any other trading vehicles. Going beyond the amount present in the trading account of commodities futures due to the limitless trading. The infamous reputation of the market is given to it by the leverage attribute, about which we already learned before. Rather, the truth is that due to trading in this market within a short period, many futures traders have faced bankruptcy and got a huge amount on them as the due amount to be paid.

It's time to understand and discuss the commodity futures trading risks involved:

Unlimited Liability

Unlimited liability exposure to the trading account is seen as one of the main facts, which needs to be faced with futures trading. In simple terms, accruing losses, which are pretty high as compared to the capital of investment. The losses will keep on increasing or getting accumulated till the time either direction is continuously followed by the chosen asset.

A small percentage known as the "initial margin", which is important for deciding and booking a position in the commodities futures, needs to be accounted for as the position value while trading in the market of commodities futures, which is unlike and in contrast with the option trading in which only the amount of money each trade has investment of is seen as a loss.

The loss if any is faced, the amount gets deducted from the initial margin, later to which when the extremely low initial margin is seen, a margin call is made. The broker would need to be paid the loss extra loss amount if the losses are huge enough and the deposited initial margin cannot cover, moreover if the amount is not paid it would eventually lead to bankruptcy.

sThe strict rules in trade placement and sound risk management practice utilization can help in managing the unlimited liability in the commodity futures market. These are the two factors, which make it even more risky for the commodity futures market newbie traders.

Leverage

Unlimited liability and having leverage have a very close bonding as we have already discussed. The commodities futures, depending on the ratio of the initial margin, can give leverage between 5 to 100 times. When the prices are moving in the predicted direction of the analysis, this proves to be an excellent option, whereas if it is the opposite, i.e. huge losses would be faced if the prices move against the prediction. Thus, as we have learned before, that leverage is definitely a double-edged sword.

Example:

After a complete fundamental and analytical analysis, the conclusion of deciding over a market direction is decided. Now, it is noticed that on an asset, which has the value of $200, the initial margin needed is just $20. Now, regardless of all the calculations and strategies, a turn in the assets is seen for the wrong and opposite side, thus taking a downfall by $20. Thus, a mere 10% low is seen in the underlying asset's price, whereas a 100% loss is faced on the initial margin. This is the way, it becomes nearly impossible for the futures market traders to invest all the things in just a single futures trading position because the risk of losses is always accompanied with the leverage.

The controls of the dollar values for each trade investment are with the positioning sizing. Thus they play a vital role.

Geopolitical Risk

One of the inherent risks of commodities trading is the Geopolitical Risk. The risk is because multiple continents hold the various natural resources around the world, plus numerous jurisdictions by the companies, foreign governments, and other independent entities have been placed.

Example:
The Persian Gulf holds in abundance, most of the oil needed by various nations for their economy. Thus, these middle-east countries need to be negotiated with by the oil companies for their oil supply.
The economic welfare of the entire nation can suffer due to these negotiations, which might get intense and cause disagreements. Environmental concern, licensing agreements, tax, and many more complex issues of nature are involved in these disagreements.

These countries can kick out companies those are not beneficial to a country, which has strong commodities control, which might be a commodity, which various nations require, easily. No magic formula is available for protection against this risk. Investing in companies with the economy and large-scale experience is the most effective way for risk exposure minimization. The risk can be managed easily by companies, which have a long track record in geopolitical dealings, whereas the companies that do not have prior experience may incur further losses than the former. Thus, this is the key factor always to consider in the commodities market.

Speculative Risk

Through speculation on a price direction in commodities, many investors look for earning big bucks quickly within a short span of time in the commodities market, which hold the risk of letting the markets move in various haywire directions. The markets can be highly volatile, despite of the fact that beneficial liquidity for the traders is provided by the speculators. Similarly, as seen in the housing bubble and the dot.com phenomenon, these speculators can see a loss in the control of this area. Therefore, cautiousness should be seen as to what evident speculation is needed in the market of commodities. Some detrimental effects may happen when commodities futures market is introduced to many speculative funds. On spotting speculation activity, which is unusual, trading in the markets should be avoided for a long time. Re-entering the markets is only possible when volatility has subsided.

Fraudulent Activities

As an investor of commodities, risk is brought in by too many factors. Adding more to this, the possibility of fraudulent activity is also there. The possibility of becoming a victim of fraud is possible, despite the commissions set for commodity futures trading, which is used and has been set for regulating the markets exchange activities.

Preventing oneself from being a victim to this risk can be done through researching before hand about the companies where the investment is being made. There are moments where fraudulent activities cannot be ignored despite of huge discipline and risk followed. There is no big deal about it, rather it's a simple game of trading, and this has to be accepted easily without any doubts over it.

Chapter 9: How to Develop a Good Commodities Trading Plan?

Developing a unique strategy in order to become a successful trader of commodities futures can be done through discussing 7 steps related to it, which definitely are easy to learn and understand them in not more than 7 days. Rather these seven steps should help in understanding commodities trading within 7 hours.

Step One: The Line of Start

Creating a plan is the first step for any business plan to work. Professional traders, with the investment capability of the total capital amount, do the formulation of a trading plan. The type of market should be understood before investing any amount with a broker. Thus the investment capital and success are directly related to each other. The probability of making a higher range of money can take place only when investment funds are higher.

The question should be asked to oneself, as to what should be the initial or the lowest trading amount to start with?

The average amount of $10,000 is recommended by the expert professionals to begin with, and it is considered as the magic number, thus is the recommended amount. To cover up the losses, which might be faced or in order to create some high profits a substantial amount is needed, which furthermore lets the trader survive and stay afloat in the market for longer durations. It is basically luck if success is seen on placing investment in trade, which is lower than the magic number. A large capital volume is needed to function so that proper risk management principles can be practiced.

The capital invested will be "at risk", is an important factor to remember and consider while investing. The amount of money needed for paying monthly bills and expenses should not be the amount used for investing, as the amount invested should make no difference or hamper the life and expenses needed for daily life.

Commodities trading account should be considered as a business, and the simple fact of life is that a huge number of businesses fail while trying to be successful. A mind, which is extremely string and sharp is needed for trading within this market of commodities. The most important part of being a successful investor of commodities futures is the fact that losses should be faced without any fear of losses or let that hinder the life prospects.

Step 2: The markets that will be traded in

Keeping the knowledge of what securities should be traded in within the market comes as the second step of creating a successful commodities trading plan. Some strict speculations can be allowed in approx. 40 futures markets due to the high liquidity they possess. Finding a market, which fits the trading method, account size, and risk level is the thumb rule for protection against high risk factors. Portfolio diversification should be done once the decision on choosing the market is made according to the preference suitability. The date and time of the large price movements taking place in the market every year is always unknown in advance. Higher probability of getting some of these opportunities can be achieved through diversification, in order to trade commodities successfully. The history that each market holds helps in deciding upon the large trending movements of markets. It is best to maximize the advantages of trends by the right market choice which are likely to grow, even though, trends would be a friend till the end.

The securities that most investors choose from the four different commodities sectors, which have a certain set of securities in each. The list is as with the most preferred sectors listed with them:

- Agriculture: Corn, Oats, Soybean, and Cotton
- Food: Coffee, Sugar and Orange juice
- Energy: Heating oil, Natural gas, and Crude oil.
- Metals: Copper, Gold, and Silver

Now lets understand the technical and fundamental analysis for deciding trade positions, as the knowledge about which markets to invest in has been learned to an extent.

Step 3: Technical & Fundamental Analysis

Investors use two methods to analyze and forecast the growth of future trend of stocks and various other aspects, and Technical Analysis and Fundamental analysis are two terms used in reference to this. Growth and promoters for each of these methods are present, just like seen in other investment strategies.

Fundamental Analysis:

In order to perform intrinsic value of an asset, attempted measurement, this method is used. Study of the whole picture can be achieved by this methodology of analysis; i.e. economic welfare, industrial conditions and also specific companies management.

Technical Analysis:

Statistics generated by the activity markets, i.e. price trends and historical volume, is used for studying the securities with using this analytical method. Technical analysts instead of using a securities intrinsic value, charts and pattern are used to find the trends and patterns which might help in deciding over the price movements, which might be possible.

None of them is better than the other in any terms; rather their advantages are against each other. Technical analysis sees the bend towards it while commodities' trading is done, reason being one of the best ways for a beginner to start trading due to the advantage it has to offer for being pretty easy than fundamental analysis, and not because it is considered to be superior in the market. A move towards fundamental analysis can be done once the comfort factor is achieved with technical analysis where the supply and demand interaction will be learned and also the commodities market price faces due to it.

History proves itself true and repeats itself is amongst the main technical analysis principles. Some identifiable pattern principles of the past reoccur which may decide on the future price movements, which might be possible can be foreshadowed. In order to forecast the future price, movements can be seen with these patterns of the chart to observe the commodities' chart. Some chart pattern is non-reliable, while some are pretty reliable.

These chart patterns can be successful mostly but still fail despite the probability of success, it's just that 100% success guarantee is not given by them. Awareness and cautiousness by the trader is important to see if the trade chart has given some incorrect analysis signs. Increasing the analysis accuracy trades entry and exit from the market are possible through this support and lines of resistance in the market.

Different methods of technical analysis, measuring the price action with the use of the study, identifying trends and increasing the accuracy of trades with precision is definitely needed to be handled for becoming a better chart analyst. The illusion for the randomness of the market will disappear once these concepts are understood completely.

Google search for "commodity charts" can be found and used to understand the commodity market analysis; various websites would appear offering charts for different required commodities.

Step 4: The Trend is Your Friend

Although, this step is a part of step 3, but due to its effectiveness towards a strategy of trading makes it deserve its own place as another step. Larger long term potential profits are offered with trading with trends, since the true market direction is being followed instead of possible predictions of what might happen.

The feeling of missing on some important ride or entering the trend late might be felt a lot of times. Thus a particular time frame should be noticed to be sure of the correct entry with confidence.
Example:

Monthly, two weeks, or daily time frames should be considered while identifying a trend. Thus this would make decision making assured by specific time frame adherence.

Long term periods are stemmed for better-produced results time frames over the time again and again, even though trends are seen in every time frame. Larger profits are gained with longer holding time periods. Short-term trends are less stable when and as compared to the trends, which last for months. Successful profits in the long term can be locked in successfully, as long as the correct judgments and money management is used.

Step 5: Losses should be cut short

Getting profits through commodities trading has one aspect as following the trend. Now the question, which crops up is that if profits are not earned, what might be the right exit time from the trades?
Before any open trade position is closed, every trader would like to gain some profits, but even more important is the fact that money should not see any loss, and yes due to ego being hurt, stopping a trade is really difficult. The

reason is that one must realize their mistake in the wrong decision-making is not an easy task. This characteristic needs to be overcome for becoming successful professional traders in the market, by accepting the fact that the market might give losses in the game of trading. The strategies which are the most polished can also face losses, is a fact that these professional traders completely understand, thus, they are successful only because they do not let couple of losses or accepting their mistake make a difference to them or let themselves suffer due to it.

This attitude of accepting losses will only strengthen the mind and heart over facing losses and make the trader understand that losses are not supposed to be the end of the world. The best profit making way is to make the losses get as minimum as possible when compared to the investment account in total. The depletion of the trading capital needs to be maintained in order to continue the commodity-trading career. Trading in the correct overall trend direction can make large profits. Large profits can be continued to enjoy as long as the capital does not deplete from the account, which is possible only when large losses are not faced.

Few losses will definitely be faced, irrespective of the method adopted for market trading, which needs to be understood through the law of probability. One of the losses will definitely be there to hurt the size of the account if a large amount of money had to be invested from the capital for all the trades.

Exiting Trades and reducing losses is possible through a number of complex ways, but irrespective of the situation the trader is in, receiving some loss while exiting the market definitely has some or the other benefit in the market. Using good stop losses and limiting the losses faced by money management skills, plus knowing how trades in the future can be used as a compensation for these losses is an important part of the trade here.

Step 6: Lets Profits take a run

This and the fourth step can be correlated. The advantage of a trend can be taken for earning accounts money can be taken if the investor has some really nice trade which has a strong trend and accumulates profits at a nice rate. The utilization of these opportunities must be made to the maximum as the duration of days, weeks or maybe months can be seen for such strong trends.

As discussed before, long-term trends can carry risks. Professional investors use a method called a trailing shop in order to counter this situation. At a small distance behind the position of trade, this trailing shop is placed, which acts as a level of the exit point. The open position can earn profits till the time the predicted direction movement of the trade is seen as a continuous approach. The trailing stop would automatically quit the trade when and if the market price direction sees a retracement in its direction. The profits accumulated from the trade are locked, and the account can be protected from huge losses, thus giving a situation for the dual winning scenario.

Step 7: Manage your risk

Managing risk in each trade is the final step for commodity market trading. We discussed the risks that can be faced in the Chapter 4 of this book, but now let's talk about the protection to risk exposure.

The things, which can be done for managing your risk in small frames, are:
- The losses as compared to the profits should be small.
- The markets should not be over-traded.
- Each trade should have a small percentage of investment when a small account is present.
- The news holds an important position and should be paid attention to. The future price movements, which cannot be predicted by technical analysis can be foreshadowed by the news and is important to remember.
- The trading goals should be realistic; the selfish motive of trying to be a millionaire in one stroke should not be tried.
- Large and random profits can be taken over by the consistent small profits.
- A trading plan before entry into commodities market is made, should be created.
- The fact that losses would be seen should be accepted, and they should be cut short.

The risk exposure can be minimized which are being used for the commodities futures trading market if every profit made is appreciated and this suggestion are followed.

www.ingramcontent.com/pod-product-compliance
Lightning Source LLC
Chambersburg PA
CBHW082251150526
45153CB00031B/452